OUR SOLAR SYSTEM

URANUS

Susan Ring

MEDIA ENHANCED BOOKS

AV2 BY WEIGL™

ADDED VALUE • AUDIO VISUAL

www.av2books.com

AV² provides enriched content that supplements and complements this book. Weigl's AV² books strive to create inspired learning and engage young minds in a total learning experience.

Your AV² Media Enhanced books come alive with...

 Audio
Listen to sections of the book read aloud.

 Key Words
Study vocabulary, and complete a matching word activity.

 Video
Watch informative video clips.

 Quizzes
Test your knowledge.

 Embedded Weblinks
Gain additional information for research.

 Slide Show
View images and captions, and prepare a presentation.

Go to **www.av2books.com**, and enter this book's unique code.

BOOK CODE

L852494

 **Try This!**
Complete activities and hands-on experiments.

... and much, much more!

AV² by Weigl brings you media enhanced books that support active learning.

Published by AV² by Weigl
350 5th Avenue, 59th Floor
New York, NY 10118
Website: www.av2books.com   www.weigl.com

Library of Congress Cataloging-in-Publication Data
Ring, Susan.
  Uranus / Susan Ring.
     p. cm. -- (Our solar system)
  Audience: 4-6.
  Includes index.
  ISBN 978-1-62127-269-4 (hardcover : alk. paper) -- ISBN 978-1-62127-278-6 (softcover : alk. paper)
  1. Uranus (Planet)--Juvenile literature. I. Title. II. Series: Our solar system (AV2 by Weigl)
  QB681.R56 2014
  523.47--dc23

                              2012044668

Printed in the United States of America in North Mankato, Minnesota
1 2 3 4 5 6 7 8 9 0   17 16 15 14 13

032013
WEP300113

Project Coordinator Aaron Carr
Editorial BLPS Content Connections
Designer Mandy Christiansen

Contents

3

Introducing Uranus

There are three types of planets in Earth's **solar system**: rocky planets, **Gas Giants**, and **Ice Giants**. Uranus is an Ice Giant in the outer reaches of the solar system. It is a puzzling planet in many ways. It glows blue-green in the night sky. It has a very unusual tilt and spins on its side. Read on to find out more about the seventh planet from the Sun.

Uranus is surrounded by gases that give it a blue-green glow.

Uranus Facts

- Most often, a planet stands upright on its **axis**. Uranus is different. It is tilted on its side.

- Uranus is the third-largest planet in the solar system, after Jupiter and Saturn.

- Uranus has rings, but they are very hard to see. The rings are made of ice, rock, and dust.

- The **atmosphere** of Uranus is made of several gases, including hydrogen, helium, and a small amount of methane.

- The center of Uranus is made of rock and ice. This is surrounded by a deep liquid, but scientists are not sure what the liquid is.

Naming the Planet

Uranus is the only planet named after a Greek god. The others are named after Roman gods. Ancient Greeks believed that Uranus was the god of the sky. Uranus is one of the first gods in Greek **mythology**. His wife is Gaea, the goddess of Earth. In Roman mythology, Uranus is known as Caelus.

Uranus is the father of Saturn and the grandfather of Zeus, the ruler of all the gods.

Uranus's Moons

Uranus has 27 known moons. Uranus's largest moons are made of ice and rock. The smallest moons are 8–10 miles across (12–16 kilometers). Many of the surface features of Uranus's moons were formed by ice melting and freezing. This action causes the surface to crack.

Oberon and Titania are Uranus's largest moons. Cordelia is the smallest. These moons are named for characters in plays by William Shakespeare.

Titania is about 1,000 miles (1,600 km) around.

First Sightings

In 1690, an **astronomer** named John Flamsteed made the first recorded observation of Uranus. However, he did not realize that he had found a planet. For many years, people believed Uranus was a dim star.

For more than 100 years after Saturn was discovered, people believed all of the planets in the solar system had been spotted. Then, astronomer William Herschel identified Uranus as the seventh planet in 1781. It was the first planet to be discovered that was not known in ancient times.

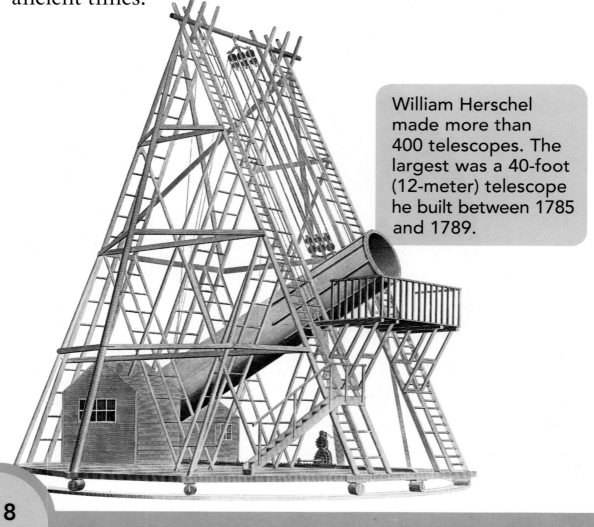

William Herschel made more than 400 telescopes. The largest was a 40-foot (12-meter) telescope he built between 1785 and 1789.

Uranus's Rings

There are 13 known rings around Uranus. The rings are made of ice boulders and dust. Scientists have also discovered smaller rings within each of the 13 main rings. These are called "ringlets."

Scientists once believed that Saturn was the only planet with rings. They were surprised when they discovered Uranus's rings.

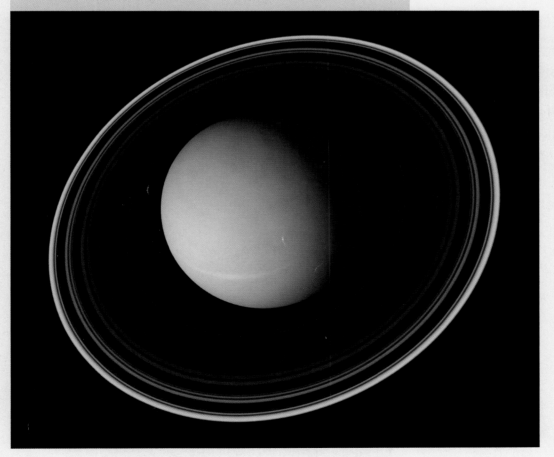

Spotting Uranus

Uranus is very far from Earth. At the closest point in its **orbit**, Uranus is about 1.7 billion miles (2.7 billion km) away from Earth. This makes Uranus difficult to see in the night sky.

The rings around Uranus are even more difficult to see. This is because the rings are very dark in color. They are some of the darkest objects in the solar system.

The Hubble Space Telescope is a very powerful telescope that has taken pictures of Uranus's rings.

See for Yourself

Uranus can be seen as a dim spec of light in the night sky. However, Uranus can only be seen without binoculars or a telescope on very clear nights. You need to know where to look for Uranus to find it in the sky. Try using a pair of binoculars if there is no telescope available.

Uranus and its moons look like a faint disks when they are viewed through a telescope from Earth. The rings around Uranus can even be seen through the powerful telescopes found at some observatories.

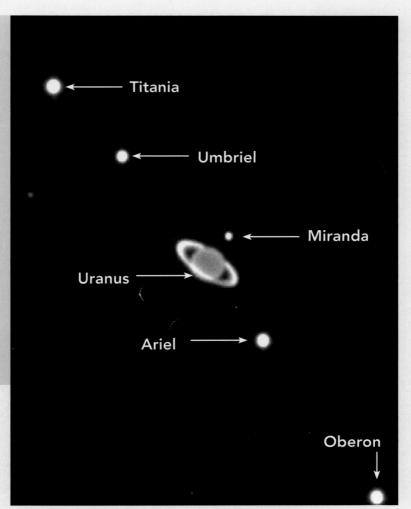

Charting Our Solar System

Earth's solar system is made up of eight planets, five known dwarf planets, and many other space objects, such as **asteroids** and **comets**. Uranus is the seventh planet from the Sun.

Sun

Mercury

Venus

Earth

Mars

Ceres

Jupiter

Order of Planets

Here is an easy way to remember the order of the planets from the Sun. Take the first letter of each planet, from Mercury to Neptune, and make it into a sentence. My Very Enthusiastic Mother Just Served Us Noodles.

Eris

Makemake

Haumea

Pluto

Uranus

Neptune

Saturn

Dwarf Planets

A dwarf planet is a round object that orbits the Sun. It is larger than an asteroid or comet but smaller than a planet.

Moons are not dwarf planets because they do not orbit the Sun directly. They orbit other planets.

Uranus and Earth

All planets in the solar system orbit the Sun. It takes about 365 days for Earth to complete an orbit. This is the length of Earth's year. Uranus is much farther from the Sun than Earth. Uranus takes longer to complete an orbit because it has a greater distance to travel. Uranus orbits the Sun once every 84 Earth years.

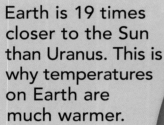

Earth is 19 times closer to the Sun than Uranus. This is why temperatures on Earth are much warmer.

Earth's diameter
7,926 miles
(12,756 km)

Uranus's diameter
31,763 miles
(51,118 km)

Comparing the Planets

Planets (by distance from the Sun)	Distance from the Sun	Days to orbit the Sun	Diameter	Length of Day	Mean Temperature
Mercury	36 million miles (58 million km)	88 Earth Days	3,032 miles (4,880 km)	1,408 hours	354°F (179°C)
Venus	67 million miles (108 million km)	225 Earth Days	7,521 miles (12,104 km)	5,832 hours	847°F (453°C)
Earth	93 million miles (150 million km)	365 Earth Days	7,926 miles (12,756 km)	24 hours	46°F (8°C)
Mars	142 million miles (228 million km)	687 Earth Days	4,217 miles (6,787 km)	24.6 hours	−82°F (−63°C)
Jupiter	484 million miles (778 million km)	4,333 Earth Days	88,732 miles (142,800 km)	10 hours	−244°F (−153°C)
Saturn	887 million miles (1,427 million km)	10,756 Earth Days	74,975 miles (120,660 km)	11 hours	−301°F (−185°C)
Uranus	1,784 million miles (2,871 million km)	30,687 Earth Days	31,763 miles (51,118 km)	17 hours	−353°F (−214°C)
Neptune	2,795 million miles (4,498 million km)	60,190 Earth Days	30,775 miles (49,528 km)	16 hours	−373°F (−225°C)

Uranus Today

Scientists have learned most of what they know about Uranus from the *Voyager 2* **space probe**. It is the only spacecraft that has flown by Uranus.

Voyager 2 was launched in 1977. First, it passed Jupiter and Saturn. It reached Uranus after nine years of travel. *Voyager 2* took 7,000 photographs of Uranus and its moons and rings. Ten new moons were found because of this mission.

Today, **NASA** uses its Hubble Space Telescope to take pictures of Uranus. These pictures show that powerful storms sometimes occur on Uranus. They show wispy clouds above the planet. These clouds move in the same direction that Uranus spins on its axis. Blowing winds make these clouds move at fast speeds. Uranus's clouds form into long bands.

Voyager 2
Launch 1977
Vehicle Flyby

Planet Watchers

William Herschel discovered Uranus

William Herschel was working as a music teacher when he discovered Uranus. In his spare time, he had built telescopes and studied the stars. He discovered the planet by accident, while he was studying stars.

Herschel's discovery made him famous. He quickly became the head astronomer for the king of England. Herschel wanted to name the planet after the king. It was named after the Greek god Uranus instead.

William Herschel spotted Uranus with a telescope that he built himself.

James Ludlow Elliot discovered Uranus's rings

In 1977, Uranus passed in front of a distant star. James Ludlow Elliot was excited to watch this event. He thought it might tell him and his team something about the remote planet's atmosphere.

Elliot and his team put a telescope on an airplane and flew above the clouds to witness the event. They observed as the star kept appearing and then disappearing. This made them realize that Uranus had rings.

James Ludlow Elliot and his team observed Uranus's rings blocking the light as they passed in front of a star.

What Have You Learned?

Take this quiz to test your knowledge of Uranus.

1 What is unusual about the way Uranus spins on its axis?

2 Uranus is a rocky planet. True or False?

3 Who discovered that Uranus was a planet rather than a star?

4 Name the only space probe that has flown by Uranus.

5 How many moons does Uranus have?

6 What is the name of the telescope that has taken many photographs of Uranus?

7 There is ice on Uranus's moons. True or False?

8 Which planet is larger, Earth or Uranus?

9 Are the rings around Uranus dark or light in color?

10 How long is one year on Uranus?

Answers

1. Uranus is tilted on its side as it spins on its axis.
2. False. Uranus is made of gases and ice.
3. William Herschel 4. Voyager 2 5. Uranus has 27 moons. 6. The Hubble Space Telescope 7. True. Uranus has several moons with ice on their surface. 8. Uranus is larger. It is four times bigger than Earth. 9. Dark. The rings around Uranus are some of the darkest objects in the solar system. 10. A year on Uranus is equal to 84 Earth years.

Young Scientists at Work

See How Uranus Spins

Uranus spins on its side. This experiment will show you how Uranus spins in space.

You will need:

- a piece of strong string, such as twine
- a long, thick needle with a large eye
- a very small orange

1. Cut a piece of string the length of your arm. Thread the string through the needle. Tie a knot around the eye of the needle with one end of the string.

2. Carefully poke the needle through the orange. Be sure to push the needle out through the other side of the fruit. Slowly pull the string through the orange until it is the same length on both sides. Remove the needle from the end of the string.

3. Grasp onto each end of the string. Hold the orange and string away from your body. Now, begin spinning the fruit by moving both ends of the string in little circles. The motion of the orange is similar to Uranus's rotation.

Key Words

asteroids: small, solid objects in space that circle the Sun

astronomer: person who studies space and its objects

atmosphere: the layer of gases surrounding a planet

axis: an imaginary line from north to south, on which a planet spins

comets: small objects in space made from dust and ice

Gas Giants: large planets made mostly of gas; Jupiter and Saturn are the two Gas Giants in the solar system

Ice Giants: very cold giant planets; Neptune and Uranus are the two Ice Giants in the solar system

mythology: stories or legends, often about gods or heroes

NASA: National Aeronautics and Space Administration; part of U.S. government responsible for space research

orbits: the nearly circular path a space object makes around other objects in space

solar system: the Sun, the planets, and other objects that move around the Sun

space probe: spacecraft used to gather information about space

Index

Log on to www.av2books.com

AV² by Weigl brings you media enhanced books that support active learning. Go to www.av2books.com, and enter the special code found on page 2 of this book. You will gain access to enriched and enhanced content that supplements and complements this book. Content includes video, audio, weblinks, quizzes, a slide show, and activities.

AV² Online Navigation

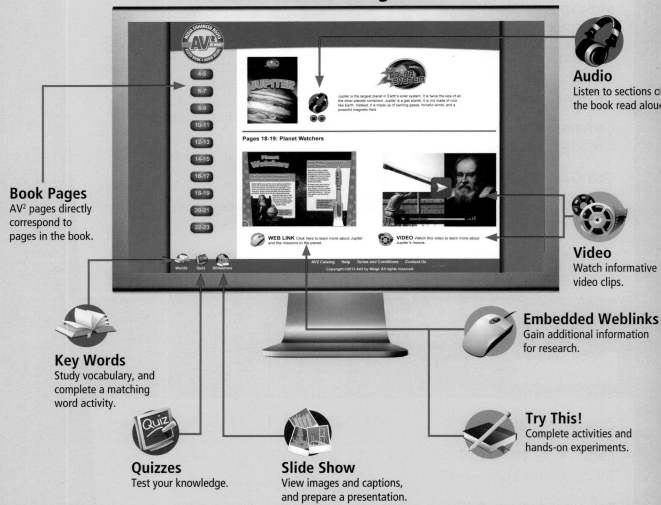

Book Pages
AV² pages directly correspond to pages in the book.

Audio
Listen to sections of the book read aloud

Video
Watch informative video clips.

Key Words
Study vocabulary, and complete a matching word activity.

Embedded Weblinks
Gain additional information for research.

Quizzes
Test your knowledge.

Slide Show
View images and captions, and prepare a presentation.

Try This!
Complete activities and hands-on experiments.

AV² was built to bridge the gap between print and digital. We encourage you to tell us what you like and what you want to see in the future.

Sign up to be an AV² Ambassador at www.av2books.com/ambassador.